HOW TO PLAY

The Absolute Basics About Badminton, Top Tips For Beginners Badminton Players

ROGER SEAN

Table of Contents

CHAPTER ONE 3

   INTRODUCTION 3

CHAPTER TWO 8

   OBJECTIVE OF THE GAME 8

   EQUIPMENT & PLAYERS 9

   THE ABSOLUTE BASICS 12

   SERVING 23

CHAPTER THREE 31

   TOP TIPS FOR BEGINNER BADMINTON PLAYERS 31

   THE END 40

CHAPTER ONE

INTRODUCTION

Badminton has been around since 16th century. Indoor play is the norm, with the Olympic Games being the pinnacle. This sport is extremely popular in Asian countries like China and India, where it is a leading trend because of their ability to produce some of the best players in the world. Badminton refers to a racquet game that uses racquets in order to hit a shuttlecock over a net. It can be played with larger groups, but the most popular forms of the game include "singles" and "doubles", which are one-player teams. Badminton can be played outdoors in a backyard or on the beach. Formal games are played indoors on a rectangular court. You score points by hitting the shuttlecock with your racquet and landing the ball within the other side's half. Each side can only hit the shuttlecock one time before it crosses the net. Each side may only strike the shuttlecock once before it passes over the net. The shuttlecock is a feathered, or (in informal matches), plastic projectile that flies differently to other balls. The shuttlecock accelerates faster because the feathers have a higher drag. The top speed of shuttlecocks is also higher than other racquet sport balls.

It is the unique nature of the sport that the shuttlecock flies.

From the battledore, and shuttlecock earlier games, this game was developed in British India. Denmark dominated European play, but the game is now very popular in Asia. Recent competitions have been dominated China. Badminton is a Summer Olympic sport that has four events. High levels of play require excellent fitness. Players need aerobic stamina and agility. They also need strength, speed, precision, and speed. It's also a technical sport that requires motor coordination as well as the ability to move racquets with precision and speed.

CHAPTER TWO

OBJECTIVE OF THE GAME

Badminton's objective is to hit the shuttlecock through the net and land it in the designated courts. A rally is when your opponent returns the shuttlecock. This rally is won by you i.e. you win a point if you force your opponent into hitting the shuttlecock out or in the net. To win a set, you must win 21 points. Most matches are best of three sets. You can win points on either serve.

EQUIPMENT & PLAYERS

There are two types of badminton: singles and doubles. It is also possible to play mixed-doubles. A stringed racket, similar to a tennis racket with a smaller head, and a shuttlecock are allowed for each player. The shuttlecock is composed of a half-round ball at its bottom and a feather-like material around the top. The shuttlecock can only be hit at the bottom. Gravity will always turn the ball side down. The shuttlecock may hit you once before it hits the ground or the net. It measures 6.1m in width and 13.4m in length. A net that runs 1.55m across the court's rectangular center is found. Two tram lines run along the court's perimeter. Two tram lines run along each side of the court. The outside line is for doubles matches, while the inside lines serve as the parameters for singles matches.

Scoring

You score a point if you hit the shuttlecock into the net and it lands in your opponent's courts before it hits it. You can also score a point if your opponent hits the shuttlecock in either the net, or outside of the parameters.

The Game is Won

You must score 21 points more than your opponent to

win a game. You will win the set if you achieve this. If the scores are tied at 20, then it is down to which player gets two clear points. If the scores are tied at 29-29, the next point will determine the winner of the set. To win the overall game, you must win 2 of the 3 sets.

THE ABSOLUTE BASICS

Badminton's goal is to hit your shuttle with your racket, so it lands in your opponent's side of the court. You win a rally when you achieve this; win enough rallies to win the match. The same goal is shared by your opponent. Your opponent will attempt to get the shuttle back to your side of the court. You can win rallies by learning from your opponent's mistakes. If he hits the shuttle under or into the net or out of the court, you will win the rally. If you believe your opponent's shot will land out then you should let it go to the floor. The rally will continue if you decide to hit the shuttle.

The rally ends when the shuttle touches the ground. Badminton, in this regard, is not like squash or tennis, where the ball bounces. The shuttle must be hit only once before it crosses the net, even in doubles. Badminton does not have multiple players who can touch the ball and then send it back over the net.

Indoor Badminton can be played

You may have played badminton at the beach or in the backyard. It's fine to play it casually, but not when you get competitive. Even the slightest breeze can cause the shuttle to drift off-course. This is why competitive badminton must be played indoors.

Establishing a badminton court

Badminton uses its own nets and posts. It is lower than volleyball. A sports centre may set up a court with a slack net volleyball net, but the staff are not trained in badminton. For proper badminton posts, and a net for badminton, ask. Three things to consider if you are attempting to setup the court yourself.

The net extends across the entire court. The net should be pulled tight and not allowed to slack. The net is located in the middle of the court so both courts halves are equal in size. It can sometimes be difficult to see the badminton court lines because other sports lines are also painted on the ground. You should focus your attention on the badminton court lines in one color.

Singles, doubles and mixed doubles

On a badminton court, you can have two or four players: one on each side or two on each. One-against one is known as singles, while two-against two is known as doubles. Doubles allows either player to hit the shuttle. You don't have to do it in turns. Only the first two shots of a rally are exceptions. I will explain this in serving.

There are five types total of badminton.

Singles for men

Singles for women

Doubles for men

Doubles for women

Mixed doubles (each pair is made up of a man or a woman).

Level doubles can also be called men's doubles or women's duplicates.

These are the only badminton types that are played in serious tournaments. However, casual play can sometimes see women playing against men (e.g. two women against two men).

What do all those lines mean?

You might think a badminton court has too many lines when you first see it. The court is marked up for singles and doubles. They use slightly different court sizes.

The doubles court is formed by the outermost lines. In a doubles rally, the shuttle can land anywhere on the court.

The singles court is slightly smaller than the doubles court. The singles sidelines are not the outermost, but the closest ones in. These narrow alleys are formed by the combination of the outermost (doubles), sidelines. These alleys are sometimes called the tramlines and side tramlines because they resemble tram tracks or train tracks. Let's think of it another way: side tramlines are in to accommodate doubles, and out to accommodate singles.

All other lines are intended for serving

We have three more lines that we need to discuss. These lines do not apply during the main rally and are only applicable when you are serving. Similar to the lines that a tennis court uses for serving, this is also true.

SERVING

Serving is the way you start the rally. Someone has to get on the shuttle first! Special restrictions on serving are in place to prevent the server from gaining an unfair advantage. They also don't apply during other parts of the rally. The receiver will be the one who takes the second shot at the rally. Doubles are prohibited because the receiver's partner cannot hit this shot.

How do you serve?

Badminton requires that the serve be struck in an upwards motion with an underarm hitting action. A tennis-style serve is not permitted. You must hit the shuttle at least three inches below your waistline. The rules specify that this must be the height at which your ribcage is lowest. You can serve a little higher than your shorts' top, but not too much.

Courts of service

The smaller boxes that make up the service courts are located inside the court. Let's first look at their purpose. The badminton court's middle line runs from the back to the net. This is the center line. The centre line of the court is intersected by a line at the front; this is called the front service line. These two lines create a T-shaped junction.

A singles court of service is a box that is made up of four lines.

The center line

A singles side line (inside side line)

The front line service line

The back line (the one that runs all the way to the back)

You have two service courts on your side: one for your right and one for your left. Your opponent will have the same service courts.

Doubles courts have slightly different service courts. They are slightly wider because they use an outside line (remember, the doubles court has a wider sideline); and they are smaller because they use an inside back line.

This is what the inside backline does: doubles service and nothing else. Because it only does one thing, it's the most confusing line in a badminton court!

Just to clarify, a court of doubles service is formed from these four lines.

The center line

A doubles side line (outside side line)

The front line service line

The within backline (not the very end, but the one that follows)

What service courts are used

Three things are served by service courts:

The server must be present in a service court.

The receiver must be in the service court diagonally to his right. The serve must be delivered to the diagonally opposite court of service. As an example, let's say the server is in his left court of service. The receiver will be in his right service court, where the serve must go. The receiver should allow the serve to fall to the ground if it is not going to land in the service court. If the receiver hits a serve, the rally will continue even though the serve was out. Both the receiver and server must remain in their boxes until the shuttle contacts them with his racket. They can then move to any court by removing the boxes.

CHAPTER THREE

TOP TIPS FOR BEGINNER BADMINTON PLAYERS

Are you a beginner in badminton or are you looking to improve your game? These are tips that will help you improve your badminton skills.

Badminton warm-up

Make sure your body is ready for badminton. Badminton requires both agility and stamina. You should focus on these areas during your warm-up. You could do some gentle jogging around the court, or skipping. When your pulse has increased and your body feels warmer, stretch all major muscle groups, focusing especially on the legs and back. This will prepare you for the lunges ahead.

The badminton grip

The grip is essential when choosing a racket. For small hands, smaller grips work best. Large grips are better for larger hands. Relax your grip when holding the racket. Flexibility in your wrist is key to achieving perfect forehand and backhand shots.

The shuttlecock flight is available.

Shuttles that 'wobble' during flight should be avoided. If a shuttle wobbles in flight, it may be on its way out or is defective and should be returned to the manufacturer or disposed off.

Maintain a central base location

After playing a shot, it is a good idea to return to your central base position. You are more likely reach opposing shots if you position yourself in the middle area of play.

Play badminton indoors

The shuttlecock was designed to be light and can be swept away by the slightest breeze. If you don't want to have to retrieve your shuttle every time, consider playing indoors.

Prepare for anything

Badminton can be unpredictable and fast-paced. You must be ready to move in any direction. It is essential to be aware of your limits. It is not a good idea to try to grab that crucial shot and end up with a painful injury.

Badminton game planning

Even though you may be a beginner, that doesn't mean

you shouldn't try some strategies. Badminton is a psychological game. Start out with little skill. Learn about your opponent's psychology so you can use their weaknesses to your advantage.

Cross-train around your badminton

Badminton is a sport that requires agility and stamina. It's advisable to engage in other activities to help your game. Jogging and Brisk

Walking are great for building all-round strength that will allow your knees to withstand the high impact of badminton. Your game will be more enjoyable if you can increase your flexibility and range-of motion by engaging in other flexibility-focused activities like yoga.

Play with your head

Badminton is a great exercise for the mind, but don't let it fool you. Although the game requires constant planning and thinking, it can be difficult for beginners to master. When you are just starting out, it is important to ensure that every shot has a purpose. Also, try to be as attentive as possible to the court at all times. Your strategy will soon fall into place. Your attitude is also important. Don't enter a match expecting to lose.

After playing, cool down

Like any other exercise, you should finish your game with a cool down. You can continue to do the same thing, but take a stroll around the court. Then, you can do some light stretching. Depending on how the game went, you might want to focus on your major muscle groups. To ensure deep stretching, hold your stretches for approximately 30 seconds.

THE END

Printed in Great Britain
by Amazon